DOUBLE

Vision

COMPANIONS

AND CHOICES

AN EXHIBITION OF QUILTS AND PAINTINGS

QUILT ARTISTS
VIRGINIA AVERY
RITA BARBER
MARIAN BROCKSCHMIDT
MARILYN DOHENY
CARYL BRYER FALLERT
PAT HOLLY & SUE NICKELS
ROBERTA HORTON
LIBBY LEHMAN
DIANA LEONE
CAROLE A. LIEBZEIT
MARY MASHUTA
PAULA NADELSTERN
YVONNE PORCELLA
JUDY SEVERSON
ANITA SHACKELFORD
RICKY TIMS
JEAN WELLS (KEENAN)

PAINTE
ROD BUF

D1472130

American Quilter's Society
P. O. Box 3290 • Paducah, KY 42002-3290
www.AQSquilt.com

Located in Paducah, Kentucky, the American Quilter's Society (AQS) is dedicated to promoting the accomplishments of today's quilters. Through its publications and events, AQS strives to honor today's quiltmakers and their work and to inspire future creativity and innovation in quiltmaking.

EDITOR: MARJORIE L. RUSSELL
GRAPHIC DESIGN: KAY BLACKBURN SMITH
COVER DESIGN: MICHAEL BUCKINGHAM
PHOTOGRAPHY: DOUG CARR

Library of Congress Cataloging-in-Publication Data
Buffington, Rod.
        Double vision--companions & choices: an exhibition of quilts &
paintings / by Rod Buffington.
        p. cm.
        ISBN 1-57432-782-8
        1. Buffington, Rod--Exhibitions. 2. Quilts--United
states--Exhibitions. 3. Artistic collaboration--United
States--Exhibitions. I. Title: Double vision--companions and choices.
II. Title.
ND1839.B767 A4 2001
709'.2--dc21.

Additional copies of this book may be ordered from the American Quilter's Society,
PO Box 3290, Paducah, KY 42002-3290, or online at www.AQSquilt.com.

To My Grandmother
Fannie Hinders Moring, 1888 – 1992,
a quilter who inspired my thought in
doing my watercolor quilt paintings.

Thank you to Rosemary, Jeffrey,
Tara, and Jill for the love you give me
each and every day. I love you.

Detail, ZINNIAS LOOKING THROUGH THE WINDOWS, Rod Buffington.

Rod Buffington

INTRODUCTION

I must begin with a thank you to the quilt artists who, three years ago, graciously agreed to participate in something unusual. That "something unusual" involved a conversation between each quilt artist and myself as a watercolor artist to develop a core concept for two independent artistic works – quilt and quilt painting.

As a watercolor quilt painter from Springfield, Illinois, I was unknown to most of the "Who's Who in Quilting" artists whom I nervously, yet boldly, approached. My proposal was that each quilt artist and I work together to design a conceptual quilt block or idea. After that, the quilt artist would take that concept and create their quilt; I would take the same concept and design a painting. Each of us could twist and turn the block any direction to achieve the overall pattern of the quilt or painting. The quilt artists were to send me samples of the fabrics they were using in their quilt for use in my companion painting, but there would be no further collaboration. Each was to see the other's work only in finished form.

My challenge was accepted by eighteen highly creative quilt artists who promised to make seventeen quilts, and *Double Vision – Companions and Choices* was born. This book showcases the results of that unusual collaboration and is a companion to the exhibit of the same name.

For this project, my painting process involved using the fabric samples provided by each quilt artist as part of the collage of the painting. All of my paintings were drawn as quilt blocks on handmade paper. Within certain areas I drew designs of fabric, then painted them with watercolor. After painting the designed areas, I collaged 100 percent cotton fabrics onto the paper within other parts or areas of the painting. Then I stitched through the paper with silk buttonhole thread.

I thank Victoria Faoro, executive director of the Museum of the American Quilter's Society, for believing in my original idea and for giving the exhibition gallery space within the museum. With this commitment, the project was elevated to a high level.

Another thank you goes to my professional friends in Springfield, especially highly-respected photographer Doug Carr, for shooting all the transparencies. Thanks also to my good friend Bob Hansen for hand building each frame for the painting pieces in the exhibition.

Now it is your turn to see if my dream for this exhibit has been realized. I leave it to you to judge whether each of the seventeen paired pieces – quilt and painting – work together to make the original idea a success, and if each can stand alone as a work of art. If this exhibit serves as an inspiration for your own work, that will be the greatest honor for all the artists represented in this exhibit.

Thank you Virginia, Rita, Marian, Marilyn, Caryl, Pat and Sue, Roberta, Libby, Diana, Carole, Mary, Paula, Yvonne, Judy, Anita, Ricky, and Jean, for the outstanding, beautiful quilts you created for the exhibition. Each of you in your own way completed the project within the parameters designed by all of us. There was never a moment of disagreement between any of us as we worked together toward completion of the project. All of you were most gracious, cooperating as I sent forms and informational papers to complete, taking time from your very busy schedules to keep this project on the front burner. In my heart I have eighteen new friends whom I will remember always. I thank you for every moment you gave toward creating and exploring to completion this very special, colorful, and creative concept. Wow!

As the *Double Vision – Companions and Choices* exhibition travels, I want to thank those individuals who have included these very creative pieces in their exhibition space, whether in a museum, gallery, or at a quilt festival. May your viewing public enjoy the show.

A very special thank you to Meredith and Bill Schroeder who agreed to publish this book. But even more than that, I thank them for their vision in establishing the beautiful Museum of the American Quilter's Society which stands as a gift to quilters and the viewing public. Your inspiration and kindness will always be remembered.

Detail, Zinnias Looking Through the Windows, Rod Buffington.

Lynn
Lewis Young

PUBLISHER / EDITOR
ART / QUILT MAGAZINE

All too frequently the world of quilting insulates itself against seeing and studying other art media. Watercolor artists likely do the same. But, from the exceptions come amazing interchanges.

Double Vision – Companions and Choices represents such an exchange. The quilts and watercolor paintings in this exhibition give the viewer visual joy and mind-expanding exploration of the interpretive differences of the artists and the two media.

Watercolorist Rod Buffington paints exactly, closely mimicking the colors of patterned fabrics and the geometry of quilt patterns in his large-scale works. He collages pieces of fabric into the designs until it is difficult to tell which is painted, which is collaged. He quilts the painted paper with silk buttonhole thread for added texture.

The quilt artists invited to participate in this duo-medium exhibit represent the full range of quiltmaking today, both in techniques used, and in style of quilt – from traditional to contemporary art quilt.

Paired together, some of the quilts and related paintings in this exhibition are remarkably similar, some quite different. Amazingly, the more "traditional" designs produced some of the most varied pairs of works. Those "in the know" about quilt design recognize there are unlimited variations of traditional designs, and that "traditional" does not mean restricted. New variations show up all the time.

In color, form, and design, the quilt and painting pairs of *Double Vision – Companions and Choices* play back and forth with variation and theme, leaving the viewer much to ponder and examine. Together the pairs say more about their conceptual beginnings than they do separately. Together they reveal more of the inherent mystery, artistic meaning, and fascination in the geometric design of the American quilt – both traditional and contemporary.

Victoria
Faoro

EXECUTIVE DIRECTOR
MUSEUM OF THE
AMERICAN QUILTER'S SOCIETY

It was summer 1998 when watercolor artist Rod Buffington visited the Museum of the American Quilter's Society (MAQS) to share with us the concept of an invitational exhibit of quilts and paintings. Rod explained that he planned to invite fifteen to eighteen nationally recognized quiltmakers to collaborate with him; each artist would create a quilt, and Rod would create a companion painting. Rod also envisioned a companion book and that the exhibit would travel to other venues after premiering at MAQS.

The quilt artists with whom he intended to work were indeed leaders in the field, and prior to approaching MAQS, Rod had secured expressions of interest from several. Rod's willingness to take on the challenge of coordinating an exhibit of this scope was admirable, especially since he was making the commitment at the same time to create at least fifteen companion paintings himself. At MAQS, we were intrigued by the idea of encouraging an interaction between quiltmakers and a painter, and by the opportunity to present an exhibit that would feature companion pieces in the two media.

Our mission as a museum is to educate about quiltmaking – to educate those who are new to the art as well as to expand opportunities for those who are accomplished in the field. What Rod proposed seemed an especially appropriate project. Rather than translating someone else's art into a quilt (which is what quiltmaker/

painter projects sometimes involve), for this project quilt-makers and a painter were going to develop ideas together and then independently create their art.

We hoped that the resulting exhibit would provide museum visitors with a better understanding of the process of creating. We wanted viewers to explore similarities and differences in detail when they encountered two pieces that shared an initial design. In some cases the initial design was an actual image, in other cases fabric pieces, but we wanted viewers to connect the two. In the process, they would develop greater understanding of how different artists can take the same materials or ideas and work with them in different mediums, creating personal expressions.

Bringing together quilts with paintings would also have an additional significance. Quiltmaking has seldom been seen as connected with painting or other two-dimensional arts. Rod's plan was to bring the two together. In the process of creating his paintings he, in fact, played with the line between fiber and paint – even occasionally collaging pieces of fabric and then creating additional pieces in paint.

This exhibit comes at a time when many quiltmakers are blurring the lines themselves, turning parts of their quilts and sometimes its entire surface, into a canvas for dye painting and other surface design.

MAQS thanks Rod Buffington for his vision and for making this exhibit available. Thanks also to the very accomplished artists who created such wonderful works for the exhibit. And finally, thanks to quiltmakers around the world for continuing to make working with contemporary quilt exhibits such an exciting endeavor.

Double Vision – Companions and Choices has proven to be even more exciting than we had anticipated, and MAQS is very proud to be the first to present this exhibit and accompanying book to the public.

Donna
Wilder

PRESIDENT
FREE SPIRIT® FABRICS

*D*ouble Vision is double pleasure!

Unlike the usual result of double vision, Rod Buffington's exhibition enables us to focus on two distinct images created from one conceptual quilt design. *Double Vision – Companions and Choices* highlights both the quilt and the painting. The results are as fascinating and diverse as the artists who created them. Yet the individual quilts, outstanding as they may be, represent but a single piece by the quilt artist, whereas Rod alone has amassed a body of work worthy of recognition – no small task for a person as busy as Buffington!

Working from a block jointly conceived with the quilt artist, Rod intricately developed his watercolor and fabric collage paintings. His art pieces arouse a familiar comfort level, yet when set against the stark white background, appear quite sophisticated. MATISSE IN MOTION, SWIRLING MOVEMENTS WITH CIRCLES, and THE E-MAN RUNNING THROUGH THE STARS, although clearly influenced by his recognition and understanding of the artist's signature style, maintain an orderly format characteristic of Buffington's work. The surprising results of BLOOMING HIBISCUS, PINWHEEL AND STARS III, MERGING LINE MOVEMENTS, and ANGLES WITHIN SQUARES, illustrate the diversity of this exhibition and at the same time the versatility of Rod's work. Through careful use of color, style, line, and design, Rod's interpretations of quilt blocks come together as strong pieces both independently and in concert with their companion quilt.

The quality of this exhibition is a credit to Buffington and to the talented quilt artists whose works are featured. *Double Vision – Companions and Choices* is a visual experience that awakens the imagination as it pleases the crowd.

QUILTED BY KATHY SANDBACH

VIRGINIA AVERY

Matisse Meets
the Millennium

56" x 57" QUILT

ROD BUFFINGTON

Matisse
in Motion

40" x 40" PAINTING

9

QUILTED BY CECELIA M. PURCIFUL

RITA BARBER

Fragments of
Women's Lives

70" x 71" QUILT

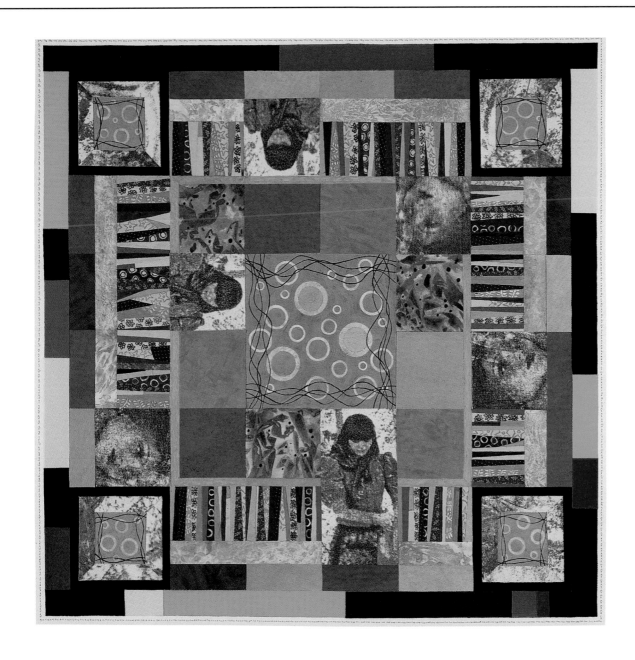

ROD BUFFINGTON

Untitled

40" x 40" PAINTING

MARIAN BROCKSCHMIDT

Logging
Lincoln

58" x 58" QUILT

12

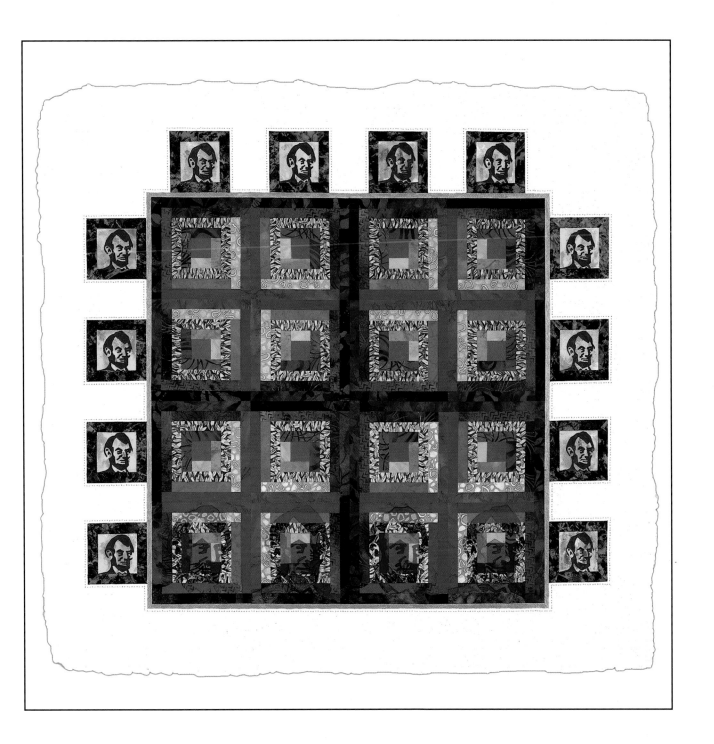

ROD BUFFINGTON

Sixteen
Abrahams

40" x 40" PAINTING

QUILTED BY JEANNIE BREWSTER

MARILYN DOHENY

Jasmine's
Peacock Fans

59" x 83" QUILT

ROD BUFFINGTON

Cubic Ribbon Fans

40" x 40" PAINTING

15

CARYL BRYER FALLERT

Interaction
#1

59" x 59" QUILT

ROD BUFFINGTON

Swirling Movements with Circles

40" x 40" PAINTING

17

PAT HOLLY AND SUE NICKELS

New York
State of Mind

69" x 69" QUILT

ROD BUFFINGTON

Twisting Curves

40" x 40" PAINTING

QUILTED BY JANET DOLLAND

ROBERTA HORTON

Baskets
for Usha

66" x 66" QUILT

ROD BUFFINGTON

Block
Baskets

40" x 40" PAINTING

LIBBY LEHMAN

Mornington

58" x 58" QUILT

ROD BUFFINGTON

Angles Within
Squares

40" x 40" PAINTING

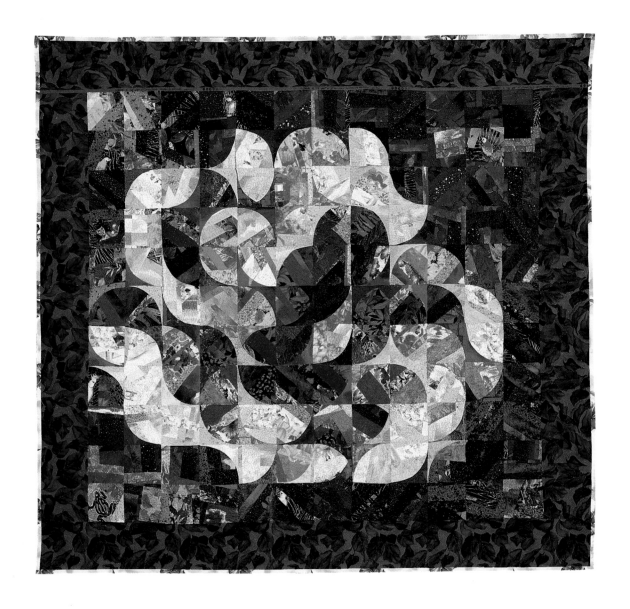

DIANA LEONE

Aloha
Hibiscus

60" x 60" QUILT

ROD BUFFINGTON

Blooming
Hibiscus

40" x 40" PAINTING

QUILTED BY DIDI SALVATIERRA

CAROLE A. LIEBZEIT

Hot
Salsa

60" x 60" QUILT

ROD BUFFINGTON

Pinwheel and Stars III

40" x 40" PAINTING

MARY MASHUTA

Roundabout
Dots

60" x 60" QUILT

ROD BUFFINGTON

Explosive Dots
Within Squares

40" x 40" PAINTING

PAULA NADELSTERN

Kaleidoscopic XXIII:
Cathy's Quilt

37" x 37" QUILT

ROD BUFFINGTON

Within the
Kaleidoscopic Scope

40" x 40" PAINTING

31

YVONNE PORCELLA

e-man
@2000.com

39" x 39" QUILT

ROD BUFFINGTON

The E-man Running
Through the Stars

40" x 40" PAINTING

QUILTED BY TONI FISHER

JUDY SEVERSON

Monarch

83" x 83" QUILT

ROD BUFFINGTON

Rings of Orange

40" x 40" PAINTING

ANITA SHACKELFORD

Rainforest
Reflections

60" x 60" QUILT

36

ROD BUFFINGTON

Four
Seasons

40" x 40" PAINTING

RICKY TIMS

Harmonic Convergence
#28: Dreamscape

83" x 57" QUILT

ROD BUFFINGTON

Merging Line
Movements

40" x 40" PAINTING

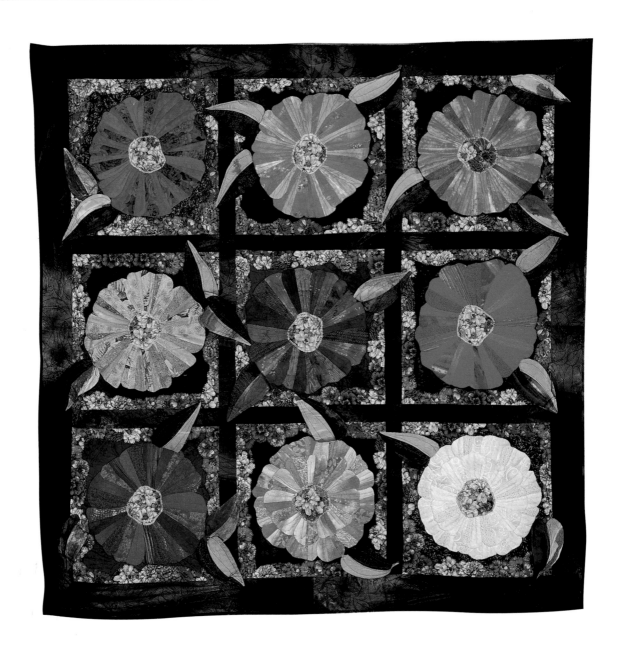

JEAN WELLS (KEENAN)

Zinnias

60" x 60" QUILT

ROD BUFFINGTON

Zinnias Looking
Through the Windows

40" x 40" PAINTING

41

Jonathan Holstein

Shared quilting enterprises have a long history in this country. The quilting bee, one of a number of work-sharing communal efforts common in an earlier America, has become a famous (if somewhat romanticized) part of our quilt-making lore. While shared quilting might have sped up the production of a finished quilt, the quilt's art came primarily from the individual enterprise of designing and sewing the top and establishing the quilting patterns.

The exhibition, *Double Vision – Companions and Choices*, is quite a different sort of collaborative effort. Since 1980, Rod Buffington has been creating a continuing and evolving series of watercolor and fabric collages based primarily on block quilt designs. For this exhibition, he invited eighteen well-known quilt artists (two worked together on one quilt) to each create with him a conceptual block. Then, each quilt artist was to create a quilt using that block as a design basis in some form while Buffington created one of his paintings using the same block as a foundation for his imagery – thus seventeen quilts, and seventeen paintings.

Collaboration between Buffington and the artist occurred only at the beginning – a starting imagistic or conceptual point from which each artist's work would develop. At the inception, it was stipulated that neither the quilt artist nor Buffington would see the other's work until it was completed. Each of the quilt artists agreed, however, to provide Buffington pieces of the material they were using so he could incorporate them into his designs.

Buffington's paintings are a combination of simulated fabric prints rendered in watercolor, and actual fabrics applied in collage fashion. He modifies some of the fabrics by painting on them, and also adds lines of silk stitching. His overall forms normally mirror the aesthetic characteristics of block-style quilts, while his work method mimics the making of traditional crazy quilts, with their amalgams of different fabrics, overpainting and decorative, non-functional stitchery. (Interestingly, Robert Shaw in *The Art Quilt* asserts: "In both intention and unrestricted creative exuberance ...the Victorian-era crazy quilt is arguably the most direct ancestor of the art quilt."[1])

I think the primary consideration Buffington deals with in making successful paintings of quilt blocks is one of proportion and scale. Quiltmakers often manipulate the size of blocks to achieve aesthetic ends. Some nineteenth century appliqué quilts have as few as four huge identical blocks forming the surface of the quilt, while some pieced quilts may have hundreds of tiny repeated blocks. Both can work successfully within the framework of quilts originally designed in scale for beds. With quilt art, the element of our expectations can be added to the normal problem of scale and imagery proportions within a frame. When the traditional design format of the block quilt is applied to making quilts of smaller scale such as crib quilts (which would be about the size of one of Buffington's paintings) or doll quilts, one cannot simply assemble fewer blocks scaled for a full-sized quilt and achieve a successful aesthetic result. Somehow, it always looks a little, or a lot, off.[2] Nor is it a matter of simply making the blocks smaller to achieve a satisfying result. Successful smaller quilts may use large, medium, or small blocks, but those blocks are somehow scaled in relation to each other and to the external frame to gain a visually pleasing result. Buffington's problem is thus multifold: how to overcome our expectations of quilt scale, and how to scale a block up or down so that it works visually within the 40 by 40 inch size he chose for these paintings. In other words, he began with a set frame size and then had to make many of the same aesthetic decisions as would a quiltmaker. In his paintings for this exhibition, as in others of his works, Buffington moved in both directions in terms of scale. In some cases he created works that at first appear to be composed of a single, elaborated block; in others he mimics, in smaller scale, the overall surfaces of both traditional block-style and appliqué quilts, and the overall painterly formats of some contemporary quilt artists.

The works of the eighteen accomplished quilt artists in this exhibition represent a number of distinctive styles developed in the course of each artist's career. Some begin their work within a traditional quilt aesthetic framework; others start with a format more traditionally seen in Western painting. The questions of scale within their chosen frameworks were, of course, very similar to the questions Buffington needed to answer, and the results in many cases are strikingly similar. As in Buffington's paintings, a few of the quilts designed and made for this exhibition appear, at least at first, to be large-scale studies of a single block, others are in a more traditional block style, others are largely painterly.

The disruption and reshaping of traditional quilt forms is, of course, very much a part of the evolving history of the art quilt. Quilt artist Yvonne Porcella began as a weaver and thus had no initial commitment to the quilt form and its attendant assumptions. She has worked in both the traditional frame, as in her work in this exhibition, E-MAN@2000.COM, and in works that draw from other traditional formats, as in her kimono-shaped pieces.[3] Kimonos represent ingenious, untailored garments shaped from uncut textile widths. They can be taken apart, cleaned, and reassembled, going from garment to bolt to garment again. In a twist on the plot, Porcella has made kimonos in both normal and oversized versions, and has mimicked the form but changed the construction method. Thus in one work she altered two traditional textile norms – the quilt and the kimono. Her quilt shares with

Buffington's painting the image of a running man pieced of cloth fragments – a commentary on the relentless urgency of contemporary life. Buffington's accompanying painting, THE E-MAN RUNNING THROUGH THE STARS, borrows a number of Porcella's pictorial devices – bright colors, checkerboard sections, energetic and visually active compositions – so there is an interesting visual and intellectual interplay between the two works.

Other quilts leaning toward a more painterly form and format are those of Virginia Avery, Marilyn Doheny, Caryl Bryer Fallert, and Ricky Tims. The common images picked by Buffington and Avery for this exhibition are silhouettes of male and female dancers and tropical foliage, derived, as Avery notes in her statement, from "…one of my favorite sources of inspiration…the cut paper work of Matisse…" Avery is an accomplished musician, particularly interested in jazz; motifs from that musical genre appear in her work. Avery's MATISSE MEETS THE MILLENNIUM is one of two quilts in the exhibition with figurative elements. In it, the powerful, basic colors of Matisse's images have been noted in a border and a bright red heart, reminiscent of the (usually) red squares that visually center Log Cabin blocks. The images themselves have been rendered in monochromatic tones, giving them a photographic quality, freezing their exuberant movement in space and time. The major form and color components of both quilt and painting are so similar that the graphic artist and the quilt artist must have decided on a broad overall approach to the theme. In this case, Buffington's work, MATISSE IN MOTION, resembles a finished drawing for the painting manifested in Avery's quilt, but both painting and drawing can stand as finished and self-contained works.

The spread fan motif common to Marilyn Doheny's quilt, JASMINE'S PEACOCK FANS, and Buffington's painting, CUBIC RIBBON FANS, is a showcase for Doheny's well-known interwoven ribbon and dimensional designs. Vivid against a monochromatic center, the spread fans tumble the length of her quilt, breaking through a rigid inner border on all sides and mingling their active designs with those of a busy wide outer border – reminiscent of French cotton prints of the early nineteenth century in its exotic riot of motifs and colors. Doheny's investigation of the fan form in her quilt moves from a realistic, flat representation to fragmented studies, some with the illusion of three dimensions. Doheny's quilt successfully balances complex fan forms on a surface that combines a calm center with an exuberant border. The result is Oriental in its evocation of exotic imagery. Buffington's accompanying painting uses hotter, brighter colors for its fan images and the composition is more formal, pulling six three-dimensional-effect studies into a tight circle centered on another illusionary image of three-dimensional boxes floating on a ribbon-woven grid. The allusions to quilt imagery (Tumbling Blocks at the center and a resemblance of the overall composition to a Dresden Plate block) tie Buffington's painting, more than Doheny's quilt, to traditional quilt design.

A sense of visual illusion is also apparent in Ricky Tims's work, HARMONIC CONVERGENCE #28: DREAMSCAPE, which floats a framed grid of rigid bars over a swirling background mass of color with tornado shapes. Interior imagery mimics views of far-distant cosmic events. Tims's bars move in a color gradation from red to blue, echoing the natural light spectrum that both reveals the shapes of things and hides from us forms embodied in wavelengths we cannot perceive. Buffington's response to the grid imagery is quite startling, and (as in his response to the image he shares with Doheny) is more rooted in quilt imagery than is the work of the quiltmaker. Buffington sees an Amish Bars quilt, but forms the grid within a framework of a typical Amish Diamond quilt, using the traditional corner blocks as visual anchors, and breaks within the bars to form the inner diamond. There is a further allusion to Amish Bars quilts in some of the solid bars, and in those flanked on each side by thinner bars, to the rare Amish Bars quilts with that configuration. Buffington's colors are reminiscent of the lush, saturated tones we associate with classic Lancaster County Amish quilts.

In Caryl Bryer Fallert's quilt, INTERACTION #1, we move from the macrocosmic images of Ricky Tims's work to the swirl of creation in microcosm – tendrils of brilliant colors with attached seeds and ova that reflect a sub-surface, microscopic plant and animal world. Fallert's forms move over a central grid with quilted reflections of their movement – densely packed and tightly coiled images that suggest the fecundity of the oceans. This sense is heightened by the way the forms move in a ballet of particles from the edges to meet in a counterpoint of creation at the center, overlaying two dark forms that suggest the division of a one-celled creature. Buffington's response to the same imagery in his painting, SWIRLING MOVEMENTS WITH CIRCLES, is more formal and conservative, with colors that are more restrained and hold mostly to the blue spectrum. In his painting we seem to be looking within the process, at the inner workings of microscopic creatures. But Buffington holds the tendrils within a containing frame, giving it a border of circles that look like the planets in a dream universe, thus carrying the image from the *micro*cosmic back to the *macro*cosmic.

Three other quilt artists, Rita Barber, Diana Leone, and Anita Shackelford, made works that seem to owe less to traditional quilt design than Buffington's accompanying paintings. Rita Barber's FRAGMENTS OF WOMEN'S LIVES, the least conventional shape of any of the exhibition's quilts, compresses cut and cropped photo-like images of women within a field of sharp, threatening glass fragments. An outer border of fragments is particularly menacing – shards in paper airplane shapes fly toward vulnerable images at the center like a concerted attack of robot planes. The whole is set on a dark night sky background, with shooting star traceries of bright quilting lines. While roughly square, its irregular edges echo the fractured chaos within; it seems much like a page ripped from an old black-paged photo album. Barber's quilt elicits a palpable sense of isolation and confinement, danger and dissolution. Buffington chose to use the imagery in a very different way. His painting, UNTITLED, puts the shared images of young women into one of the oldest and most traditional quilt formats – the center medallion – complete with fancy traditional center, corner blocks that echo it, and inner borders. The human images become part of the overall visual fabric of the quilt, merging with a form that carries a strong traditional connotation in quilters' minds. Thus the menace and angst present in Barber's quilt is missing from Buffington's painting.

Floral imagery, a traditional mainstay of American pieced and appliqué quilts, supplies the motif in several works. Diana Leone's ALOHA HIBISCUS uses fabrics printed after her watercolor designs. It centers an expanded, abstract hibiscus flower, built of Sea Shell blocks with sinuous curved sections, on a blue and green tropical grid teeming with vegetation. Other hints of a tropical paradise are in little figurative images – a parrot, a frog, a cockatoo, and a smiling Eve-like beauty who appears to be offering fruit. An outer border of shocking red has dark leaf-like images, and a final binding shows an occasional peek of pink flowers. The offset center is reminiscent of the creative chaos and unpredictability of the tropics with a riot of colors and forms. In his accompanying painting, BLOOMING HIBISCUS, Buffington uses the floral image in a more traditional manner. Sixteen squares composed to look like strip crazy blocks are each centered in a bloom – pink on the outside blocks, yellow for the four center squares. Buffington's border is more evocative of the deep night sky than the world of tropical colors, but the wonderful variety of greens in the blocks creates an appropriate setting for the rich blooms.

Tropical imagery also informs Anita Shackelford's RAINFOREST REFLECTIONS, which positions cutwork floral images like those in traditional appliqué quilts on an undulating pieced field of fat, snake-like forms reminiscent of well-fed anacondas. Hot colors, mottled light, and the sensuous lines of the rainforest juxtaposed with appliquéd shapes as reminiscent of snowflakes as of tropical foliage, carry the surprise of a contradictory event. Buffington's accompanying painting, FOUR SEASONS, is an interesting counterpoise. His format is more derivative of traditional quilts – four large blocks with appliqué imagery. But the images themselves, set on a stark white background, are, in their colors and forms, both more tropical than Shackelford's images and more traditional, reflecting the bold colors and prints of the pre-aniline cottons of appliqué quilts from the first half of the nineteenth century.

Powerful floral imagery animates another quilt and its accompanying painting. In ZINNIAS, Jean Wells (Keenan) placed nine powerful flower images within a block format. Yet their leaves, not so easily tamed, break through the sashing. The quilt resembles the sort of serial imagery investigated by pop artists such as Andy Warhol (who did, in fact, do a series of large floral paintings). The extremely rich surface of ZINNIAS – flowers with centers surrounded by strong colors and lush materials – is held within a mulch-colored border quilted with complex leaf patterns. In his painting, ZINNIAS LOOKING THROUGH THE WINDOW, Buffington uses a profusion of realistically portrayed blossoms contained in rectangular boxes and grids, but without the regulating format imposed by the block structure. The result is a work that might

have been a collage done from seed catalog photos, with blooms impossible in their perfection. The palette is nostalgic, reminiscent of the colors of appliqué quilts from the 1930s.

Four of the quilt artists, Carole Liebzeit, Libby Lehman, Mary Mashuta, and Paula Nadelstern, worked in traditional formats modified through color and form manipulations. Liebzeit's HOT SALSA makes reference to some of the earliest pieced traditions with its center medallion, blocks in Pinwheel and Variable Star designs among others, and a Sawtooth border. But the hues (Lancaster Amish quilt colors on acid) and the mixed but balanced block imagery, bring it forward in time. Buffington in his painting, PINWHEEL AND STARS III, employed some of the same imagery in a less traditional format, creating a frame on his paper then pushing forms through its boundaries. His colors, while lively, are somewhat more conservative than Liebzeit's. In both works there is an energetic thrusting of forms towards the corners.

In MORNINGTON, Libby Lehman's typically simply forms are foils for the rich surfaces she creates through color manipulations and complex drawings in thread. Her quilt makes a gesture toward traditional form in its overall structure and blocks, but these are manipulated to form a thoroughly contemporary and cerebral statement through a variety of subtle and visually interesting surface devices. An underlying surface web of organic lines mocks the rigid geometry of the blocks, creating a powerful visual tension. In handling the simple shared block imagery in his accompanying ANGLES WITHIN SQUARES, Buffington created perhaps his most playful painting in the exhibition. Repeated block elements are scattered over the surface in a manner that suggests an exploding pieced quilt. It has a pleasing lightness of spirit.

At first glance, Mary Mashuta's ROUNDABOUT DOTS appears to be an exuberant version of a traditional format. She has, however, done a nice turn on the style, creating a work that looks more like an op art painting than a quilt. Optical illusion quilt designs like Baby's Blocks are, of course, instructive in working tonal variations in materials to create dimensional effects (as in this case, must have been Nancy Crow's March Study of 1979). Through a clever and successful manipulation of form, Mashuta's quilt achieves the visual effect of a rising pyramid of blocks that triggers a dimensional message in a primitive corner of our brains. The work is also a visual thesis on polka dots; they add significant energy to the composition. Buffington's EXPLOSIVE DOTS WITHIN SQUARES, uses the circle and dot motif in quite a different way, breaking the surface into a grid of small blocks with polka dotted serpent-like forms winding through it – a landscape of fantastic shapes and colors – benign snakes from a Technicolor dream. It is by far the most active surface he created for the exhibition, and one would like to see more of the same.

Like others of Paula Nadelstern's quilts, the design of KALEIDOSCOPE XXIII: CATHY'S QUILT, is derived from the complex visual patterns produced by a three-mirror kaleidoscope. As Nadelstern explains, the optical device produces "…a complex symmetry with repetitive patterns merging triangular and square shapes." When the forms are interpreted in rich golds, reds, and blues, and then organized in a block format with sinuous sashing, the overall result is one of impossibly complex, arabesque stained glass, illuminated with a golden light. The quilt successfully forms in fabric the often fleeting, magical, and beautifully illuminated images viewed through kaleidoscopes. Buffington choose an almost literal interpretation of a kaleidoscopic image for WITHIN THE KALEIDOSCOPIC SCOPE. Centered on a circular paper, the image hovers in space, reminding one of the peculiar sensation of seeing, within a tube, the passage of an endless number of changing, symmetrical images – all magical, and all pleasing to the eye.

Five of the artists in the exhibition – Marian Brockschmidt, Sue Nickels, Pat Holly, Roberta Horton, and Judy Severson – created their work in traditional formats, colors, and imagery. Brockschmidt's LOGGING LINCOLN, uses small Log Cabin blocks positioned to form broad bands of light and dark across the quilt, and floats four ghostly images of the martyred president on its surface. Positioned in the lighter bands, the portraits seem illuminated by a pale light. Tightly composed, the quilt has a quiet dignity befitting its subject. Buffington in his painting, SIXTEEN ABRAHAMS, used the same elements, Log Cabin blocks and portraits of Lincoln, to quite different effect. The same partially obscured images of Lincoln peer from the bottom row of blocks. Other Lincoln images, in sharp detail, project in a regular procession along three sides of the central image's border, a number of them washed with red in a reminder of the passions and bloodshed that led to Lincoln's tragic end. It is Lincoln as pop icon, the image in our pocket on the $5 bill, and in our national consciousness.

Sisters Pat Holly and Sue Nickels draw inspiration for the quilts they create together from a side of the American quilt tradition they distinguish as "folk quilts," a term easier to identify than define. NEW YORK STATE OF MIND exhibits the exuberant forms and colors, the simplified, stylized, and appealing imagery, and inherent dynamism of American folk art. The New York Beauty block they chose is a triumph of American piecing architecture with a strong "folk" feeling and a good deal of internal energy. Their work is not, of course, a literal copy of a New York Beauty quilt. Instead, they took the block's basic elements and, in a study of the design idea of both block and quilt, transformed them into a large central block. Surrounding borders and corner blocks hold imagery one usually sees in the exuberant appliqué quilts of the mid-nineteenth century. NEW YORK STATE OF MIND's combination of orange, red, and green colors are strictly Pennsylvania. Buffington uses the image in TWISTING CURVES to create a work that looks more like a traditional quilt than does NEW YORK STATE OF MIND. Although Buffington chose colors similar to those employed by Holly and Nickels, his grid of blocks gives a fair idea of how the design might work when New York Beauty blocks are combined in a quilt. With its powerful form, color, and confident composition, it is a particularly successful painting.

Roberta Horton's homage to a traditional style in BASKETS FOR USHA uses modern handmade cottons from India and fabrics of her own design to create a Baskets quilt marvelously evocative of the mid-nineteenth century in style and color. This is a considerable feat given the distinctive colors and prints of that period, especially the unmistakable pre-aniline hues. The compositional balance and elegance of Horton's work is particularly appealing and successful. Horton has anchored the corners of her quilt with Nine Patch blocks (one of the great design inventions) in two merging shades of brown – ghost images of the brighter files of blocks between. Buffington's response to the baskets image, BLOCK BASKETS, is an abstracted version that breaks the image into its constituent parts and works those parts into his painting in various guises and combinations. His colors are a mixture of the old and the new, the 1840s and the 1940s, historically incongruous but not artistically – the influence is pure Nancy Crow.

Judy Severson's initial inspiration grew from her study of the great appliqué chintz quilts of the earlier nineteenth century. Her own broderie perse-style quilts are evocative of this tradition, but are distinctly updated. Her quilt for this exhibition, MONARCH, retains the formality and conservative format of the earlier tradition – a framed center with inner and outer borders. But the exuberance of flowers and butterflies, and the odd but pleasing juxtaposition of highly colored and monochromatic floral imagery, would have been foreign to the sensibilities of the 1800s. Buffington's use of floral imagery in his accompanying RINGS OF ORANGE owes less to the traditions of the nineteenth century than to the nostalgic imagery of this century. The five framed floral wreaths at the center of his composition look like cards for some sentimental occasion (Mother's Day perhaps?) and may, in fact, be an allusion to the quilt cards Severson designs. But Buffington's images are surrounded and contained by a border with mixed monochromatic and floral imagery similar to that in Severson's quilt, and, as in her quilt, it rings a strange and interesting visual note.

When artists labor together on aesthetic projects, they give up some of the magic of their privacy for the potentially synergistic benefits of cooperative work. And in some cases their labors are rewarded, the whole becoming more than its parts. The aesthetic issues raised and illustrated in the works prepared for the exhibition, *Double Vision – Companions and Choices,* are a bonus for those interested in such things, and I think quiltmakers will be among them.

Jonathan Holstein

Footnotes

[1] Shaw, Robert, *The Art Quilt*. Hugh Lauter Levin Associates, Inc., 1997, p. 42.

[2] It is almost always apparent when a larger quilt has been cut down to make a crib quilt, usually done because crib quilts are often more valued in the antiques marketplace. Even when old cloth and thread are used to make a fairly authentic looking "old" binding, the inappropriateness of the scale is usually immediately evident; it just looks wrong.

[3] Miriam Schapiro's well-known 50-foot long painting/collage, "Anatomy of a Kimono," explored this subject matter brilliantly in the 1970s.

MATISSE MEETS THE MILLENNIUM

Virginia Avery

PORT CHESTER, NEW YORK

My creative art is centered on fabric and jazz! I say "fabric," because the word encompasses both quilts and wearable art, and in one way or another I've been heavily involved with both all my life. I learned to sew when hardly big enough to reach the pedal of mother's treadle sewing machine. A world of trial and error later, I am still consumed by fabric.

I learned to play the piano by listening. Somehow the music comes out through my fingers, although I never learned to read music along the way. I was lucky to live at a time when jazz was ubiquitous, for to me quilting and jazz are intertwined in my life and in my art. I love the spontaneous improvisation of jazz, and I use the same approach when I'm working on a quilt or on a garment. I really don't plan ahead, for I never know what will happen.

For this project, I fell back on one of my favorite sources of inspiration – the cut paper work of Matisse. When I first saw Matisse's cutouts at the National Gallery in Washington, D.C., I was blown away, completely unprepared for such brilliant color, such whimsical and seductive shapes, and my responding feelings of joy, energy, and improvisation. It has influenced a lot of my work! As I looked at Matisse's work, rather than seeing painted shapes, I saw fabric appliqué, and it was dynamite!

In this quilt, MATISSE MEETS THE MILLENNIUM, I wanted to convey a sense of joy and abandon. The feeling of improvisation is highlighted by the use of black and white fabrics throughout the main section of the quilt. I adore appliqué in all its forms, but I prefer a curved line to a straight one. As long as the points don't have to meet, I will piece fabric. Making a repeat block quilt would be disastrous for me, for no two blocks would be the same. My approach to sewing is too spontaneous and too impulsive for such precision. However, my bow to tradition is in the border, in chevron piecing, but it is balanced by a blaze of color in primary and jewel tones. I love color, and it is as powerful in jazz as it is in quilts and clothing. It sets the mood. Matisse (I'd like to think!) might be dancing in his grave. ∎

Virginia Avery's works began appearing in major exhibitions in the early 1980s. Recognized in 1994 as a leader in the quilt world, Avery was also recognized by Mirabella *magazine as one of the country's 1000 most influential women.*

46

FRAGMENTS OF WOMEN'S LIVES

Rita Barber

CARLINVILLE, ILLINOIS

Since childhood I have played with color and design in whatever form I found at hand. Although I have done needlework since I was a small child, literally learning at my maternal grandmother's knee, I didn't do my first quilting until 1962, when I was expecting my first child. Quilting has provided me with both an avocation and a vocation, and my life is wonderfully intertwined with quilting.

My work ranges from very traditional to the type of work expressed in this piece – whatever approach it takes to express a particular idea. Fragments of the work began to form in the mid-'70s with the purchase of the fabric which has the images of women. It was intended for a quilt from the moment of purchase. Over the years, it was taken out and examined and many more pieces of fabric were added to the tote bag in which it lived. It was just never ready to "be" a quilt, although it had its name from the day I bought it.

My thought upon first seeing this fabric was, "how like women's lives it is – bits, pieces, fragments, all put together to make the design on the cloth." The quilt expands that idea with the use of one each of the images as they appear in the fabric.

Then fragmented images are used, each with its own identifying companion fabric, to tie whole image and fragmented images to each other. The theme is further expanded by using more brightly colored fabrics representing a variety of significant events that blend with muted colors to represent the whole of life. Fragments in a life are also represented by the manner in which the various fabrics have come to me, and what I've learned from those from whom the fabrics have come.

The quilt includes commercial fabrics, both purchased and given to me by many friends and acquaintances – hand-dyed fabrics from Judi Warren and Milly Churbuck of Country House Cottons, hand-printed fabrics from David K. Small, artistic fabrics by Small Expressions, and some hand-painted fabrics I did myself. It was constructed with "fragments" of many techniques and materials, both old and new. ■

Spanning over four decades, the works of Rita Barber draw on a variety of inspirations and employ numerous techniques to achieve a design concept. She is also an entrepreneur of quilt exhibitions in the United States.

47

Marian Brockschmidt

SPRINGFIELD, ILLINOIS

Quilts have always been a part of my life. During the years of the Great Depression, my mother, widowed at age 39, made quilts from the scraps left over from the many dresses she made for me and my three sisters. These quilts were used on our beds. My younger sister and I also accompanied my mother as she participated weekly in quilting at our church. I have fond memories of playing under the quilts, and of enjoying the coffee cake refreshments.

I learned to embroider at the age of 8 and when about 10 years old, mother had me buttonhole stitch around her Butterfly quilt. My first attempt at quiltmaking was an appliquéd baby quilt kit; mother quilted it for me in 1943. After her death in 1948, a favorite aunt quilted some youth-sized quilts for me and introduced me to quilting on a hoop. Since then I have quilted all my quilts, by hand, on a hoop. I also quilt around a big frame with the ladies of my church.

My quilts are largely adaptations of traditional and commer-cial patterns with a few of my own designs. Although a few have been machine pieced, the majority are pieced or appliquéd and quilted by hand. In 1986, I took a workshop taught by Elly Sienkiewicz and became intrigued with Baltimore quilts. Presently, I am making my eighth Baltimore type quilt using Elly's patterns from her Baltimore album quilt books and some of my own designs. These quilts have been made for wedding gifts for my grandchildren and great-grandchildren.

Having made 85 quilts, my prayer is that the Lord will continue to bless me with good eyesight and the use of my hands, so I can reach my goal of making 100 quilts in my lifetime. ∎

Marian Brockschmidt's quilts have been blue ribbon winners at Illinois State Fairs since 1974. Regarded as Illinois's quiltmaking treasures, Brockschmidt's works have been featured extensively in publications, television programs, and exhibitions.

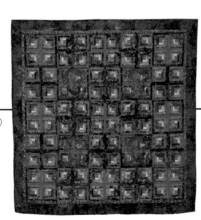

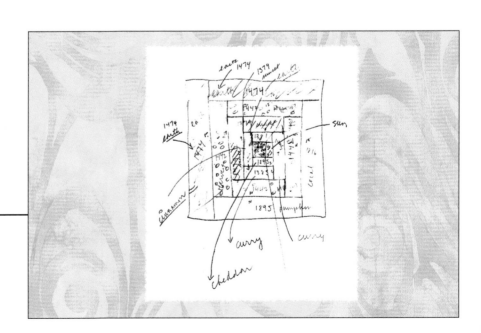

JASMINE'S PEACOCK FANS

Marilyn Doheny

EDMONDS, WASHINGTON

I've always been both a people person and a fabric person. In 1982, when the first of my three children was 9 months old, I desperately needed an outlet with a lot of adult interaction. So, to save my sanity, and to work with fabric, I enrolled in a six-week basic quiltmaking class. During the course, each student was to piece one Pinwheel potholder using a single triangle template, then quilt it, and bind it. That was the beginning of quilting for me.

I never finished that potholder, although it does hang "in progress" on my sewing room wall, proving that great things can come from humble beginnings. From that moment I was hooked and I began to search the public libraries for books of quilt patterns. In the process I discovered that there are shapes other than triangles, and was sudden-

ly and overwhelmingly in love with the endless possibilities!

Since then, my life has included every aspect of quiltmaking, from creating my own quilts to teaching others about the art. I've made hundreds of quilt tops and as I teach, I hope I've inspired others to experience the same joy I do. Dreams never die – there are always new patterns to design and innovative sewing techniques to discover. The things that give purpose to the joys of my life are color, texture, fabric, geometric patterns, and people. ■

Marilyn Doheny is an author, quilt and fabric designer, teacher, and publisher. Recently Marilyn created her own line of 47 unique fabrics, called Treasures of the Gypsies, for Northcott Silks.

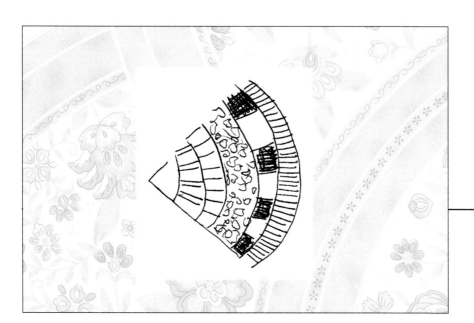

Caryl Bryer Fallert

OSWEGO, ILLINOIS

For as long as I can remember, I have expressed myself through artwork. My formal training was primarily in design, drawing, and studio painting. After many years of painting, sewing, and experimenting with other media, I discovered that fabric, as an artistic medium, best expressed my personal vision. I love the tactile qualities of cloth, and the unlimited color range made possible by hand dyeing and painting.

For the last 17 years, I have been a quilt maker (i.e., my work is constructed from layers of fabric, stitched together). Most of my current work is made from cotton fabric, which is first hand dyed and painted, then pieced, appliquéd, embroidered, and quilted by machine. Textures are created by layering and pleating. Whole cloth quilts may be dye painted. Sometimes images are designed using a computer assisted drawing program and printed directly to cloth.

The focus of my work is on the qualities of color, line, and tex-

ture that will engage the spirit and emotions of the viewer, developing a sense of mystery, excitement, or joy. Illusions of movement, depth, and luminosity are common to most of my work.

Both my geometric color studies and my more organic two-dimensional abstracts are inspired by visual impressions collected in my travels, in my everyday life, and in my imagination. My work is about seeing, experiencing, and imagining rather than a pictorial representation of any specific object or species.

I intend for my quilts to be seen and enjoyed by others. It is my hope that they will lift the spirits and delight the eye. ∎

Caryl Bryer Fallert's work has been exhibited extensively throughout North America, Europe, Japan, and the nations of the Pacific Rim. She is a three-time winner of the coveted American Quilter's Society Best of Show Award.

NEW YORK STATE OF MIND

Pat Holly & Sue Nickels

MUSKEGON, MICHIGAN and ANN ARBOR, MICHIGAN

Quiltmaking is an expression of creativity combined with a connection to women of the past. We are inspired by antique quilts and draw from their sense of design. Our quilts are contemporary versions of pieced and appliquéd antique folk quilts. To us, the naive and whimsical approach to design used by these quiltmakers is captivating.

We use machine techniques to construct our quilts. At an early age, sewing skills were acquired from our talented seamstress mother. Our technical abilities are equal and we feel very comfortable working on joint projects. Over the years, we have developed a cohesive working relationship. From the design concept, to fabric shopping, to actual construction, we share in all aspects of each quilt's construction. Our choice of materials include 100% cotton fabrics, threads, and batting. Fusible web is used in most of our appliqué, with a blanket stitch to enclose the raw edges. Freemotion work is our choice of machine quilting techniques. Using today's technology is a wonderful way to continue the traditions of quiltmaking.

Our educational backgrounds include science, health, art history, graphic design, and fine art. All of this influences how we approach quilt design and color choices. We receive many comments on our color choices and believe our experiences contribute to those decisions. Color is what draws the viewer to the quilt and because of that, when beginning a quilt project, we regard color of primary importance. For design ideas we turn to antique quilts and textiles. There are so many fabulous images that we never lack for inspiration. We do not copy a quilt exactly but use one or two elements to create our own original work.

We hope to continue our joint efforts and create quilts that will be a tribute to the past and an inspiration to future quilters. ∎

Sisters Pat Holly (right) and Sue Nickels (left) are recognized as innovative contemporary quilt artists both individually and as a dynamic duo. Their inspiration comes both from traditional quilts and contemporary music.

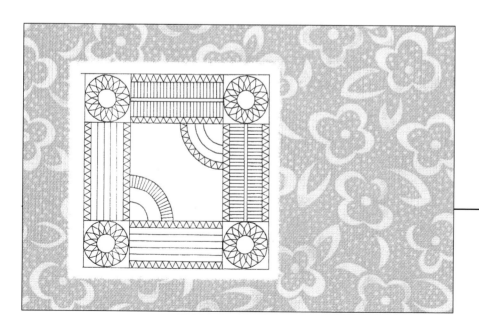

Roberta Horton

BERKELEY, CALIFORNIA

My first effort with needle and thread was in rendering a pre-printed design on a linen towel when I was 10 years old. In the fifth grade I moved on to sew clothes for my doll. By seventh grade I was making my own clothes. Knitting was added as a skill in the eighth grade. My sewing projects were made from commercial patterns, the sweater from a kit. I had no idea that I could create my own projects from start to finish, but I did know that I loved working with textiles.

I became a quiltmaker in 1970 after attending my first quilt event. Upon walking into that quilt-filled room, I knew that this was what I wanted to do. Within two years, I was teaching quiltmaking and in 1973, taught the first state-accredited quilt class in California through an adult education program.

I had a voracious appetite to learn everything I could about quilts and to explore new possibilities. I also had the desire to share that information through my teaching; ultimately I authored six quiltmaking books that are summaries of what I have learned along the way. Teaching is one of the ways that I creatively express myself – making quilts is the other.

My work is very much influenced by antique quilts, although I don't always work in a repeat block format. Fabric selection seems to be the most important part of the process for me. My goal is to have my quilt be a showcase for the fabric. I want those pieces of yardage to tell me what to do with them, including how to quilt the finished piece.

My tastes are very eclectic. The textiles I use are often collected on teaching trips. The resulting quilts therefore need to capture the essence of what I saw, what I observed, and what I learned. Most of the time I include some of the handwoven plaids and stripes that I design. ■

A quiltmaker for over 30 years, Roberta Horton travels and teaches extensively worldwide. Her quilts do the same, with her works frequently featured in exhibitions across the United States, and in Europe and Asia.

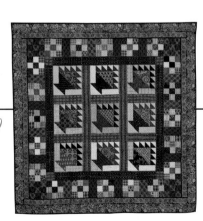

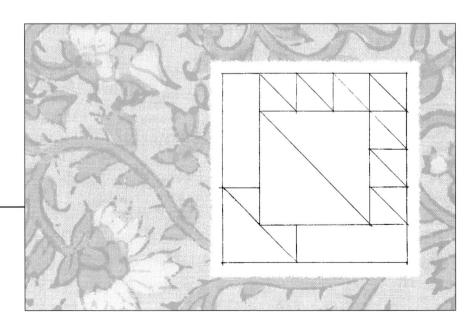

Libby Lehman

Making quilts is an utter joy for me. Although parts of the process can be tedious, the product is always worth the effort. I cannot imagine not making quilts; they are an integral part of my life. The making of quilts is woven through my days in much the same way as are reading, sleeping, or visiting with friends. Having a home studio allows me to work for five minutes or for hours on end. I like the freedom to come and go, to work in spurts or for longer periods as I choose. What a luxury!

I work on one quilt at a time, from start to finish ("finish" means the slides are taken and in the notebook). This discipline helps me focus in on each quilt as a distinct entity. It also cuts down on the clutter, both literally and figuratively.

Part of my creative process involves an ongoing dialogue with my quilts; too many voices trying to talk at once would be distracting. It usually takes from a few days to a month to complete a quilt.

Being a studio art quiltmaker has given me experiences and opportunities I would never have had otherwise. I am very grateful for the chance to share my quilts with others in the hope that they will touch a chord somewhere in kindred souls. ■

From Germany to Japan and across the United States, Libby Lehman's quilts have achieved honor everywhere they have been exhibited. Known for her unique use of threads, she is also an inspiring author, teacher, and quiltmaker.

ALOHA HIBISCUS
Diana Leone
SANTA CLARA, CALIFORNIA

It's been a long journey, but as I look back over the years, I find I've been involved in every aspect of quiltmaking. These days I travel extensively, teaching and writing. I've also owned a quilt shop. Most recently, though, my interests have revolved around creating fabric designs for Northcott-Monarch, Toronto. I've also designed fabric lines for P & B Fabrics and Kona Bay. These fabric lines are available through quilt shops worldwide.

Teaching has taken me to many places in this country and throughout the world. Twice I've been invited to Japan as a teacher, and was the first American instructor to teach quilt students and crafts teachers in Japan, introducing American patchwork to Japan in 1978. Teaching quilting has taken me to Germany, Switzerland, France, Canada, Australia, and the United States.

Most of the time I work from my studio in Santa Clara, California. I do make quilts and prefer making contemporary quilts in a style I developed – impressions of the memories of places I've seen. My quilts have been exhibited widely; my quilt, ICE, is currently traveling with the *Quilt National Exhibit*. I've been privileged to work internationally with Viking Husqvarna and Bernina sewing machine companies. As a teacher for both companies, it is exciting to market machines to quilters. For 25 years, quilting has been an important part of my life and I have thoroughly enjoyed the journey. ■

Diana Leone opened the first U.S. quilt shop in 1974 and wrote the first quiltmaking textbook for beginners in 1979. Always a groundbreaker, she has curated international quilt exhibitions and has seen her work featured and honored worldwide as well.

Carole A. Liebzeit

WILSON, WYOMING

"Traditional with a twist" and "stretch your boundaries" are how I describe my approach to quilts, wall art, wearables, and teaching. I love color interaction and try to use rich, joyful colors and embellishments. Many of my pieces have manipulated segments, beads, buttons, embroidery threads, and cording – all added to build up a textured surface.

My background as a potter taught me that creatively and from a construction point of view, I want my quilts to have more than meets the casual eye. Balance and harmony are essentials in whatever I do.

I enjoy frequent international travel and collecting textiles from other cultures has influenced my personal work and motivates my lectures and teaching. Living in both the Middle East and Europe has offered me the opportunity to explore textile museums, visit sources of tribal art, and also make rich new friends within the wonderful world of cloth.

I try to maintain a "hands on" style of interactive teaching.

Students are able to see a constant turnover of class samples illustrating new color combinations and new ways to create a more interesting surface – whether it be with manipulated fabric or the addition of embellishments. Regardless of their skill levels, I want to expand their individual horizons. A whole new world of opportunities are offered in the idea that traditional blocks can be shifted, turned, enhanced with bold accents and embellishments, as well as jazzed up with a different palette.

As a frequent Fairfield Fashion Show designer, I've enjoyed the challenges of designing innovative garments and seeing them often featured in numerous publications. Over the years, various corporations have also commissioned works for their collections. ■

Carole Liebzeit is a quiltmaker, fashion designer, art and quilt educator, and quilt judge. Her skills extend into the fashion realm, with her wearable arts garments featured as part of the Fairfield Fashion Show since 1991.

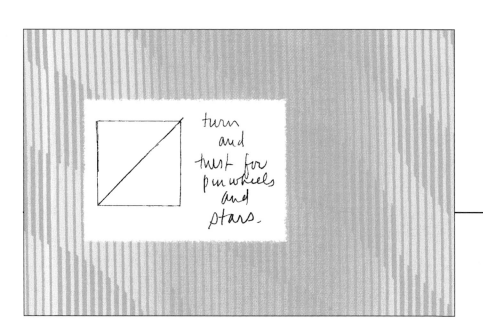

turn and twist for pinwheels and stars.

ROUNDABOUT DOTS

Mary Mashuta

BERKELEY, CALIFORNIA

I have been a quilter for 30 years and have seen many changes. Learning to quilt before there were speed methods and quick tricks to get the job done faster, I enjoy the slower process of having the quilt evolve over a period of days. Even though I often make contemporary quilts and wearables, I am still most interested in working with pieced blocks. Part of this is because I now rely on an assistant to do most of my cutting and, in this case, much of the stitching of the quilt. For me what is most exciting is collecting the fabrics, deciding on a project, and moving the cut pieces around on the design wall. The latter step is often painful and prolonged, but terribly rewarding when it all finally goes together.

I enjoy the challenge of exploring a pieced block through creating a number of quilts featuring the block. This allows me to indulge the fantasy, "What would happen if..." I am always looking for simple blocks that will show off my fabrics. The circle-within-a-circle block can be fragmented and used in many configurations. The original inspiration for this quilt layout was a 1909 embroidered fan quilt.

I accidentally amassed a dot collection before I realized what was happening. However, I knew it would be fun to see what could be done with dots as I had previously explored stripes and found them fascinating. With stripes I had discovered that the more you know, the more you can know; and the more you see, the more you can see. The same would be true of dots. This is my fourth dot quilt. It contains a selection of dot fabrics that span from the 1920s to the present.

I love being a quiltmaker today, just as much as I always have. Right now each new day brings the promise of finding the most wonderful or largest dot fabric ever made. ■

As an author, teacher, and quiltmaker, Mary Mashuta's works have been exhibited and honored worldwide. Double Vision is not her first collaborative exhibition. In 2000, her work was featured in a highly-acclaimed Smithsonian Institution exhibit that paired quilt artists with chefs.

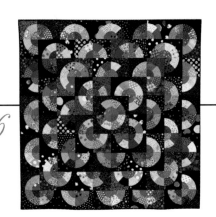

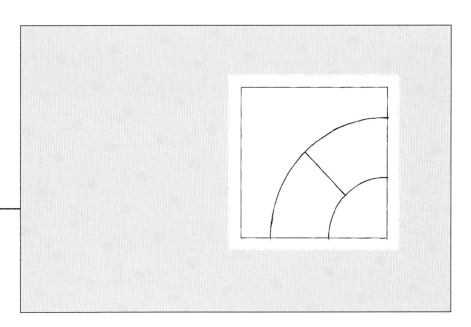

KALEIDOSCOPIC XXIII: CATHY'S QUILT

Paula Nadelstern

BRONX, NEW YORK

Kaleidoscope – the very word promises surprise and magic, change and chance. Exploding with visual excitement, a kaleidoscopic design organizes an abundance of light and color, form and motion into a complex and coherent image. My goal is to harmoniously integrate the idea of a kaleidoscope with the techniques and materials of quiltmaking. I try to free myself from a conventional sense of fabric orderliness, seeking a random quality in order to imitate the succession of chance interlinkings and endless possibilities synonymous with kaleidoscopes.

There are two kinds of surprises – the meticulously planned kind and the happy coincidence. Making kaleidoscope quilts allows me to synthesize elements of both, to merge control and spontaneity to spark something unexpected. There is a sense of "Abracadabra!" as the last seam is stitched, because the whole is truly greater than the sum of its parts. Often effects more wonderful than I imagined occur, making me both the one who makes the magic and the one who is surprised.

I work making my quilts on the very same city block in the Bronx where I grew up. Historians have suggested that the block-style method of quiltmaking evolved in response to the cramped quarters of early American life. My family's living arrangement in an urban environment created similar considerations which, unwittingly, I resolved in much the same way. My work space in our two bedroom apartment is the 40-inch round kitchen table. A long distance view, alternate space, or not making quilts are not options. I believe this reality merged with my personality and passion for fabric, shaping the direction of my kaleidoscopic piecework, causing me to rely on intricate detail and inherent symmetry, inventing a shape that makes the most of limited space. My block style method is on a pie-slice section.

Until I met quilts, I thought I was creative but not talented. To find something you love to do is a gift. To achieve recognition for it is a miracle. When I am overwhelmed by a longing for functional space, complete with a door I can close, I try to remember this. ■

Paula Nadelstern has an outstanding record of exhibitions and awards. She has authored numerous books and articles, and has been featured in media interviews and reviews in national and international publications. Her works are widely exhibited and honored.

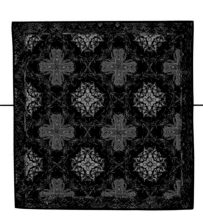

57

Yvonne Porcella

MODESTO, CALIFORNIA

The medium of cloth allows great versatility in expressing my feelings and creative ideas. I use bold colors and original designs to create a fresh approach to contemporary art quilts. I use traditional geometric piecing within this milieu and strive for innovation and new perspective.

The art quilt is the chosen medium for my artistic expression. Quiltmaking is not a family tradition – I did not learn at my grandmother's knee – rather all forms of needle arts were taught to me as a young child. My first quilt was made as a gift for a godchild. The art of patchwork was unknown to me at that time, the quilt was made using a white with floral print fabric, layered over a piece of cotton sheeting, with a backing fabric. I carefully hand quilted around each motif of the print in black thread. I had great confidence in my stitching!

The mathematics of patchwork – making blocks with complex angle pieces – is not my style. I prefer to select a theme and use cotton fabrics to make an image based on the concept. The sewing machine is my tool and I join the edges of my fabrics with a variety of stitches. The end result of the design is most important to me and the means to make that come to reality are simply the techniques necessary to accomplish the task.

As I look around, my mind is selecting fabrics for specific portions of my design and careful attention is made to how the colors and prints will combine in a pleasing way. Recently I designed a new line of fabrics and this quilt attempts to use fabric prints and colors from my new collection of fabric designs.

The concept for this quilt design began with thoughts on the turn of the century. My quest was to record the feelings of the moment as we marked the beginning of a new century. How will we approach life in the fast lane? The figure of the running man races on the path 2000, filled with urgency, movement, no time but future time. He is caught in the race of e-mail and hurry-up technology, a bit like Alice's rabbit, "Too late, too late, for a very important date!" ∎

Yvonne Porcella's outstanding art quilts are found in the collections of museums, galleries, and corporations around the world. Recognized as an innovator and leader in the quilt world, Porcella is an author and teacher who also recently designed a line of fabrics.

Judy Severson

BELVEDERE, CALIFORNIA

A friend sparked my interest in quilting by giving me one Bear's Paw quilt square and extra fabric. Together, using scissors, we cut squares and triangles, and she taught me to sew each piece together by hand. When the top was finished we took it to her local church, and members helped me stitch and baste the quilt layers. I hand quilted the quilt over a six-month period. This was my introduction to quilting in the early 1970s.

Combining quilting with printmaking, I started a business selling original embossed quilt prints and note cards. This gave me a chance for an in-depth study on the history of quilts and the women who made them. I feel strongly about quilts and the way they celebrate our past. For 20 years, I created quilt prints while quietly quilting in the evenings.

In my study of quiltmaking history, the era of chintz quilts in the 1800s was one of my favorites. The term "broderie perse" was coined in the 1900s to identify this style of quilt. It was a time when fabrics with large printed flowers in bouquets and garlands

were used. I wanted to make quilts in this style, but it was not until the early 1990s that large contemporary printed floral fabrics became available. By carefully studying the way the floral fabrics were designed, I found I could select whole groups of flowers, and create a single bouquet by placing a bow at the bottom, or by using the repeats in the fabrics. I could cut whole garlands to run the length of a border. By carefully selecting large groups of flowers to sew to my quilt top, I saved hours that would have been spent sewing one flower at a time.

The fabrics I choose are my only limits in making broderie perse quilts. There are no patterns to follow or restrict me in designing my quilts. I am free to develop a unique design for each quilt. ■

Judy Severson draws on her studies of quiltmaking history and the quilts of earlier eras for the inspiration for her broderie perse quilts. A quiltmaker for three decades, exhibitions of her works have spanned the continental United States.

Anita Shackelford

BUCYRUS, OHIO

I am sure! I've been in love with quilts since the time that I realized they existed. My grandmother's quilts and my aunt's collection of antique quilts were my early inspirations and I began making my own quilts in 1968. Quilting is both an artistic expression and a personal part of my life. I love working with the combination of color and design and the texture of the fabrics to create something new. The other reason that I quilt, and that I make large quilts, is to leave a legacy for my family – to say that I was here and to show a little bit of what my life was about.

Most of my quilts are stitched by hand in both the appliqué and the quilting. I enjoy the process and the leisurely pace of handwork. My work is almost always traditional in style, but I enjoy developing my own designs, changing or adding to the tradition to make the quilt my own. Many people associate my name with my family album quilts, which were made with a combination of dimensional appliqué and embroidery embellishment techniques. I have also put quite a bit of time into the study of many different types of raised work and stipple quilting, which can add wonderful texture to the surface of a quilt.

RAINFOREST REFLECTIONS is something of a departure from my traditional work. The curved-pieced background allows colors to flow across the surface rather than be contained by a block set. From my original offering of twelve cutwork designs, six of these designs were chosen to be used by Rod Buffington and myself in some way. My first decision was to vary the size of the motifs and then float them across the pieced background. Placing the appliqué motifs across seam lines and color changes in the background allowed for a study in comparative contrast of value, with a single color or value against several different values in the background. The quilting adds detail to the individual motifs and follows the flow of color across the piece. I have included small amounts of ruching, embroidery, trapunto, and stipple quilting in this piece, tying it to my previous work.

I love the diversity that quiltmaking offers. I'm certain that my work will always include appliqué, and I am happy that a change in style or color can allow each piece to make its own statement. ∎

Anita Shackelford is known for her traditional designs and the precision of her appliqué workmanship. A quilt artist, teacher, author, and judge, she is nationally known, honored, and exhibited.

HARMONIC CONVERGENCE #28: DREAMSCAPE

Ricky Tims

ARVADA, COLORADO

My series of harmonic convergence quilts is the result of asking the question, "What would happen if...?" What happens when two multicolored fabrics are cut into strips and converged into each other? What if that result is also cut and converged? What happens when a pieced design is cut into strips and then converged into a multicolored fabric? What happens when two surface designs are cut and converged? What happens when the strips are different sizes? For me, the possibilities seem endless and the results are extremely rewarding.

I enjoy releasing the control over the design by allowing the juxtaposition of designs to interplay, creating movement and allowing the quilt to become something other than I might have designed or expected.

I have been designing and making quilts for about 10 years now, and am delighted to share my passion, experience, and enthusiasm with quilters at every level of expertise. I find creativity in all forms to be challenging, and I want to encourage others to cultivate self-expression.

In addition to being a quilt artist, I also work as a music conductor, composer, arranger, producer, and performing artist. In recent years, my schedule has included engagements across America, Canada, and Europe, and I've developed and performed multi-media presentations that combine narrative, slides of quilts, and live music. ■

Audiences around the world recognize that Ricky Tims is a multi-talented musician, conductor, quilt artist, and performer. He crosses the lines between music and quilt art with ease, connecting afficionados of both to each other and linking the two mediums.

ZINNIAS

Jean Wells (Keenan)

SISTERS, OREGON

Fabric has held a fascination for me since I was a little girl fashioning doll clothes. It was my medium of choice for creative endeavors. To this day it allows me an outlet for pursuing my artistic side, as well as providing me the tools to make a living doing something I love. I feel very fortunate to have discovered quilting when I was in my 20s and teaching home economics. Seeing others learn, and being involved in that process, is the foundation of what I do. That foundation applies whether I am operating my growing quilt shop, The Stitchin' Post, writing how-to quilting books, or traveling the country sharing my quilting with others. Making quilts is a creative process that fascinates and energizes me. I never tire of it.

Gardening is my second passion. Much of the inspiration for my current quilts comes from the garden. I strive to capture the essence of what I see, feel, and experience in the garden since that could become the subject matter for a quilt's design. Other times it is color or the shapes in the garden that become quilting motifs. The challenge of interpreting the garden in fabric motivates me to find new piecing solutions and then share them with others.

ZINNIAS reflects my experiences in the garden, infusing color, shape, line, and design. As I did my garden chores, I studied my zinnias and their foliage, taking note of the petal shapes and arrangement, the center motifs, leaf shapes, and observing how they grow. I also enjoy these beauties in vases all over my house as well as at my store. The richness of that experience is seen in the detailing in this quilt. From conception of the idea, each part of the process has delighted me. I see the quilting stitches as the final statement.

Every quilt that I make is an experience and a reflection of what I see and want to capture in threads and fabric. Quilting holds my interest for a variety of reasons – the "hand" of the fabric, eagerly anticipating working through the design process, finding solutions along the way to help portray what I am "seeing in the garden," and stitching by hand and machine. My quilts are personal experiences that feed my soul. Quilting has allowed me a rich and productive creative existence based on sharing ideas as well as producing quilts. ■

Jean Wells (Keenan) has been an organizer of the acclaimed Sisters [Oregon] quilt show since 1975. Recognized for leadership in the quilting industry, this quilt artist, author, and owner of an award-winning quilt shop, has also seen her quilts exhibited worldwide.

Rod Buffington

My creative art pieces reflect quilt images as paintings. Although the exact compelling reason why this came to be so eludes me, I'm relatively certain that its origins are steeped in my fascination with my grandmother's quilting activities.

Quilting past the age of 93 in a lifetime of 104 years, my grandmother's delicate, colorful patchwork quilts were created with love, precision, and a commitment to making useful objects beautiful. Quilting has always turned "scraps" into magical creations with stories and imaginative names. Perhaps my grandmother's work and focus challenged me to use my own artistic skills to adapt quilt images into compositions using paint and fabric. I do know for certain that as my work continues to evolve, I embrace the challenges that it provides.

My paintings combine watercolor, designer 100% cotton fabric, and silk buttonhole thread to portray quilt images on handmade paper. I develop paintings based on historical and traditional patterns as well as my own quilt designs. Japanese rice papers are sometimes applied to unite elements.

My paintings become intricate designs through a process incorporating drawing and painting fabric designs along with collage elements of actual fabric and rice paper, then adding hand-stitched thread lines for accents. I particularly like the pristine white-on-white effect of white silk thread on the handmade paper, but I have on occasion used colored threads if the design warrants. The stitching in my paintings provides a finishing touch and a look one associates with a traditional quilt.

Each quilt composition provides a kaleidoscope of color and pattern. I use from six to nine print designs within a single quilt block – some are painted designs, others are fabric collage. Using both methods increases the illusion of depth and richness. Since I began attending the Houston International Quilt Market three years ago, I've also introduced into my work exciting new fabric designs from several major internationally known fabric companies.

As an artist, I am continually seeking new avenues to explore while refining my style. When a painting is finished, the work is matted or mounted and framed for hanging. ■

Rod Buffington has been painting watercolor collage quilt patterns since 1980, and his work has been exhibited extensively throughout the United States. A recognized leader in both civic and artistic endeavors, Buffington's unique watercolor art is widely collected and awarded.

Art is a re-evaluation of your own work – addressing the need to continually grow through your own creativity. It is understanding that your first piece of art was the best, and then understanding that your first piece of art was the worst – and that you still have not done your best work. – Rod Buffington

WATCH FOR THE

Double Vision – Companions and Choices

exhibition at the following venues:

MUSEUM OF THE AMERICAN QUILTER'S SOCIETY
PADUCAH, KENTUCKY

INTERNATIONAL QUILT MARKET AND FESTIVAL
HOUSTON, TEXAS

TARBLE ARTS CENTER
EASTERN ILLINOIS UNIVERSITY
CHARLESTON, ILLINOIS

PATCHWORK AND QUILT EXPO VIII
BARCELONA, SPAIN

PRIMEDIA GALLERY
GOLDEN, COLORADO

QUILTERS' HERITAGE CELEBRATION
LANCASTER, PENNSYLVANIA

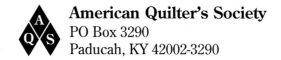

American Quilter's Society
PO Box 3290
Paducah, KY 42002-3290